◆ Personal, Moral, So
and Cultural education

GROWING UP TODAY
Relationships

Key Stage 1/P1-3

Ros Bayley and Lynn Broadbent

HOPSCOTCH
EDUCATIONAL PUBLISHING

◆ Acknowledgements

Published by Hopscotch Educational Publishing Company Ltd,
Althorpe House, Althorpe Street, Leamington Spa CV31 2AU.

© 1999 Hopscotch Educational Publishing

Written by Ros Bayley and Lynn Broadbent
Cover design by Kim Ashby
Page design by Steve Williams
Illustrated by Cathy Gilligan
Cover illustration by Cathy Gilligan
Printed by Clintplan, Southam

Ros Bayley and Lynn Broadbent hereby assert their moral right to be identified as the authors of this work in accordance with the Copyright, Designs and Patents Act, 1988.

ISBN 1-902239-16-4

All rights reserved. This book is sold subject to the condition that it shall not, by way of trade or otherwise, be lent, hired out or otherwise circulated without the publisher's prior consent in any form or binding or cover other than that in which it is published and without a similar condition, including this condition, being imposed upon the subsequent purchaser.

No part of this publication may be reproduced, stored in a retrieval system, or transmitted, in any form or by any means, electronic, mechanical photocopying, recording or otherwise, without the prior permission of the publisher, except where photocopying for educational purposes within the school or other educational establishment that has purchased this book is expressly permitted in the text.

Contents

Introduction	4
Caring for each other	6
Differences	11
Friendship	16
Families	21
Brothers and sisters	26
Responsibilities	31
Listening to each other	36
Loss and how to cope	41
Generic sheets	
Who helps us?	46
My friend	47

Introduction

It is easy to make the assumption that relationships happen naturally and that simply by engaging in them we will learn all about the process. In reality, relationships are complex and require us to bring a wide range of qualities to the process.

We need to develop listening skills, manage the delicate balance of giving and receiving and be able to interpret both our own feelings and those of others. It will be necessary for us to express ourselves effectively, being clear about our intentions, thoughts, feelings and needs.

Children will experience relationships in a variety of contexts and with varying intensity and will have to come to terms with the way in which, while some relationships are longstanding, others are linked to circumstances and are more transient in nature. Relationships are constantly changing and when they come to an end, involve us in dealing with feelings of loss and isolation.

Every relationship is unique but all relationships have to be worked at and demand that we assume certain responsibilities. Within the realm of relationships, conflict is inevitable and accepting and dealing with this conflict requires skills and attitudes that can only develop over time and require facilitation by caring, aware and sensitive adults.

Relationship skills are certainly 'caught' very effectively when children grow up with good models and it could be said that there is no better way to learn. But what if children have no access to such good models? In such circumstances we can do more than help them by taking the view that relationship skills can be taught, we can help all children in enhancing their understanding of these crucial life skills. Without these skills it can be difficult to make effective relationships and we can find ourselves isolated and without the vital companionship that we all need to lead happy and fulfilled lives.

Relationship skills are also important to our success in life. It is difficult to achieve success when we cannot make effective relationships. Successful communication with others is crucial to our well-being, we all need to be able to respond appropriately to others, without aggression or passivity.

Each chapter of this book is devoted to a different aspect of relationships and the 'focus books' have been carefully selected for their capacity to raise questions and enable children to wonder why a character did or said things and whether they were or were not right. Through this process we believe that we can help children to understand that what they do or say affects others.

The stories provide a vehicle through which the children can explore their beliefs and develop empathy for others.

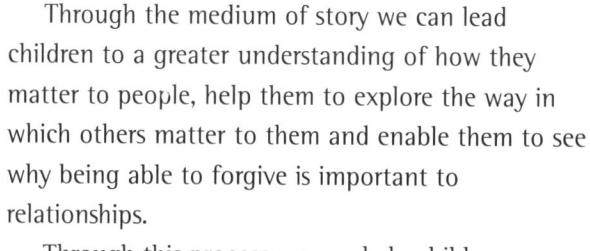

Through the medium of story we can lead children to a greater understanding of how they matter to people, help them to explore the way in which others matter to them and enable them to see why being able to forgive is important to relationships.

Through this process we can help children engage in reflection, bring the unconscious into the conscious and hopefully as a result of such work, approach their relationships more responsively and with greater sensitivity.

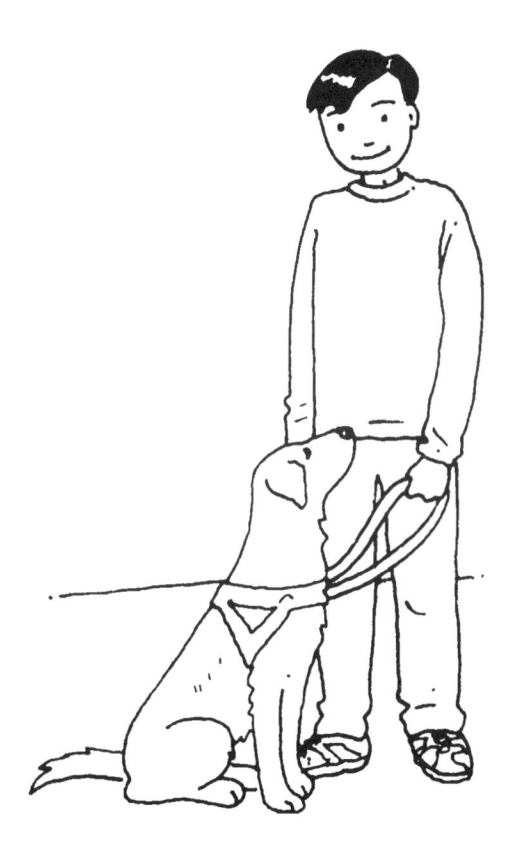

> 'People are lonely because they build walls instead of bridges.' (J F Newton)
>
> 'There are no strangers, just friends we have not yet met.' (Native American Traditional)
>
> 'The more I travelled, the more I realised that fear makes strangers of people who should be friends.' (Shirley Maclaine)

◆Caring for each other

FOCUS BOOK

ALFIE GIVES A HAND
by Shirley Hughes
Picture Lions

INTENDED LEARNING

◆ To develop a greater awareness of the ways in which we can care for and support others.
◆ To understand situations that trigger our empathy.

ANTICIPATED OUTCOMES

◆ The children will be able to talk about the ways in which they can care for and support each other.
◆ They will enhance their awareness of situations where empathy would be appropriate.

Synopsis of the story

When Alfie is invited to Bernard's birthday party he is very excited – that is, until he realises that he will be going on his own. On the day of the party he puts on clean clothes and his new shorts and sets off, taking his comfort blanket with him. All through the party he clutches the blanket tightly, never putting it down once, until Min, who is very frightened by Bernard's boisterous antics, needs his support and he abandons his blanket so that she can hold his hand.

Notes for teachers

Even very young children can sometimes have a facility for empathy that can really surprise us. This is not always apparent in classroom situations where adults are available to offer support, but in the playground, their ability to feel empathy for each other and support each other can be more easily observed.

Where children have a lack of empathy for each other, this is often because they are not conscious that someone is distressed and in need of support. This can be witnessed in the way young children will often laugh at someone in distress e.g. when they slip over or fall off a chair. They then look shocked and surprised when we register our disapproval, but if we can respond sensitively and offer them an opportunity to talk about the situation, they respond differently when similar situations occur.

Empathy is developed in a variety of contexts. Real life situations, role play situations, stories, television and theatre all offer opportunities for exploration: Alfie Gives A Hand is one such opportunity.

Methodology

Read the story with the children and allow them plenty of time to study the illustrations, as they are really important to their fully appreciating the characters' feelings. Encourage them to look closely at the facial expressions.

Questions to ask

- How did Alfie's feelings change when he realised that Mum and Annie Rose would not be at the party?
- Why did Alfie fetch his blanket? Why did he need it? Have you ever had anything special like the blanket? Allow the children to offer their anecdotes.
- What did Min need to help her feel safe?
- When Bernard put on his tiger mask Min got really upset. How did Alfie help her?
- To bring out the point that our feelings of empathy can sometimes override our fears, you might ask: "Do you think Alfie would have put down his blanket if Min had not cried?" This is a subtle point, but some children are able to appreciate and comment on it.
- Bernard's Mum told Alfie that Min would not have enjoyed the party without him. What did she mean?
- Encourage the children to relate the story to their own experience. Ask: "Have you ever had to go anywhere or do anything that made you feel very anxious or nervous? Did anyone help you? How did they do this?"
- Can you remember a time when one of your friends felt unhappy or nervous? How did you help them?
- Throughout the story Bernard is very excited and, while this is a side issue, it is one that is well worth exploring. Draw the children's attention to the range of anti-social behaviours that he engaged in. You might ask:
  – What is Bernard doing in this picture?
  – Why do you think he is behaving in this way?
  – How do you think the other children feel about the way he is behaving?

The photocopiable activity sheets

What helps you to feel safe? This sheet is intended for children who are unable to express their feelings in writing. It is primarily a speaking and listening exercise and will be enhanced by some adult facilitation.

Who could help you? This activity is essentially a thinking activity to encourage the children to look for solutions to problems. It does not require any writing skills but could be extended to include them with more able children, for example having matched the pictures they could suggest other ways of solving the problems.

How could you help? This sheet is intended for children who can write independently but could be used with younger children if an adult scribe was available.

FURTHER READING

- Mr and Mrs Pig's Evening Out by Mary Rayner (Piccolo Picture Books)

◆ What helps you to feel safe? ◆

- ◆ This little girl is going on a trip. She is taking her teddy because it helps her to feel safe.
- ◆ Talk to your friends about what they would take. Draw some pictures.

Who could help who?

◆ Cut out these pictures and match them.

PHOTOCOPIABLE PAGE

◆ How could you help? ◆

◆ Talk about these pictures with your friends.
  Choose one to write about.

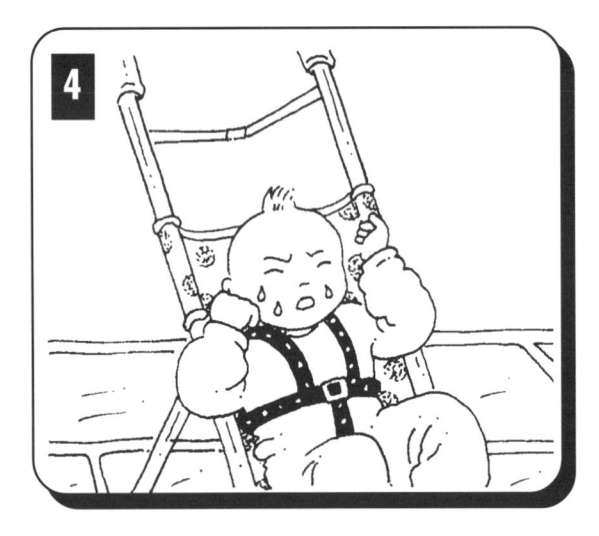

◆ I chose picture _____

✎ _____

_____

_____

_____

PHOTOCOPIABLE PAGE

◆Differences

FOCUS BOOK

BUT MARTIN
by June Counsel
Picture Corgi (Transworld)

INTENDED LEARNING

◆ To understand the ways in which we are all different and unique.
◆ To appreciate that there are experiences that are common to all of us.
◆ To understand how personal qualities can contribute to a group and be appreciated by others.

ANTICIPATED OUTCOMES

◆ The children will appreciate ways in which the children in the story are the same but also different.

Synopsis of the story

Four children are on their way to school on the first morning after the holidays. They are all very different and as they reluctantly make their way to school they meet someone who is very different indeed! Martin is a green alien who can tackle all of their school work with the greatest of ease and is more than happy to help them. Suddenly, the first day back at school doesn't seem half as bad!

Notes for teachers

But Martin focuses very directly, yet very sensitively, on the ways in which we are all different. The four children (and Martin!) are all individuals and all unique. It looks at differences in terms of gender, culture and social background and allows us to explore the ways in which we all have different physical attributes, personalities, abilities and preferences.

In sharing the book with children, we are able to consider the ways in which our individual differences can enrich the lives of others as we share our attributes and learn from each other. Although very different, the four children are firm friends who collaborate and support each other through a variety of shared experiences.

This book is particularly useful in mono-cultural schools where it is perhaps not as possible to learn about different cultures from first-hand experience. In any discussion about differences, it is important to remember that children will bring their experiences from home to the discussion and that their attitudes will reflect those of their parents. For this reason it is important that we respond to what they have to offer with great sensitivity.

Methodology

By sharing this book, we aim to help children understand that we are all different and that this is fine. Value judgements are unhelpful and should be discouraged.

Questions to ask

◆ Ask the children to look very carefully at the front cover. Ask "What do you think about the people in the picture?" Encourage them to identify the differences in terms of gender, physical appearance and so on. Get them to speculate on whether Martin is a person.

◆ How do the children feel on the first morning back at school? Do they show it in the same way?

◆ Show the picture of the four children. Match the descriptions to the appropriate face. Talk about the way in which all our faces are slightly different and ask them to relate this to themselves. This will need to be carried out sensitively, ensuring that the children's vocabulary is descriptive rather than judgemental.

◆ When Martin appeared, all the children responded differently. It is important to bring this point out and it may be helpful to ask:
 – "Why do you think Lee giggled when she saw Martin?"
 – "Why do you think Lloyd shouted?"
 – "Why did Billy whistle? What sort of whistle do you think he made?"
 – "Angela gasped, why do you think this was?"

◆ When the children first played with Martin they all did different things. To help the children understand that we all have different strengths get them to focus in the pictures, noticing the different ways in which the children played.

◆ The children in the story all go into the classroom. To appreciate the way in which we all have different aptitudes and can do different things ask:
 – Did the children all do the same work?
 – Who did the work more easily?
Bring out the way in which Martin used his ability to support the others.

The photocopiable activity sheets

My friend This sheet is aimed at encouraging the children to focus on the physical attributes of one of their friends. It involves very little writing.

We are all different This is essentially a speaking and listening activity which requires the children to elicit information from their friends. The only writing involved is that of writing friends' names.

What would they do? This sheet requires a range of skills including being able to write independently. It is aimed at older children, who should be able to complete the task with little adult intervention. The activity can be greatly enhanced by comparing the outcomes on a variety of sheets and drawing out the ways in which people respond differently to situations.

FURTHER READING

◆ Amazing Grace by Mary Hoffman and Caroline Birch (Frances Lincoln publishers)

◆ My friend ◆

◆ Draw a picture of one of your friends.

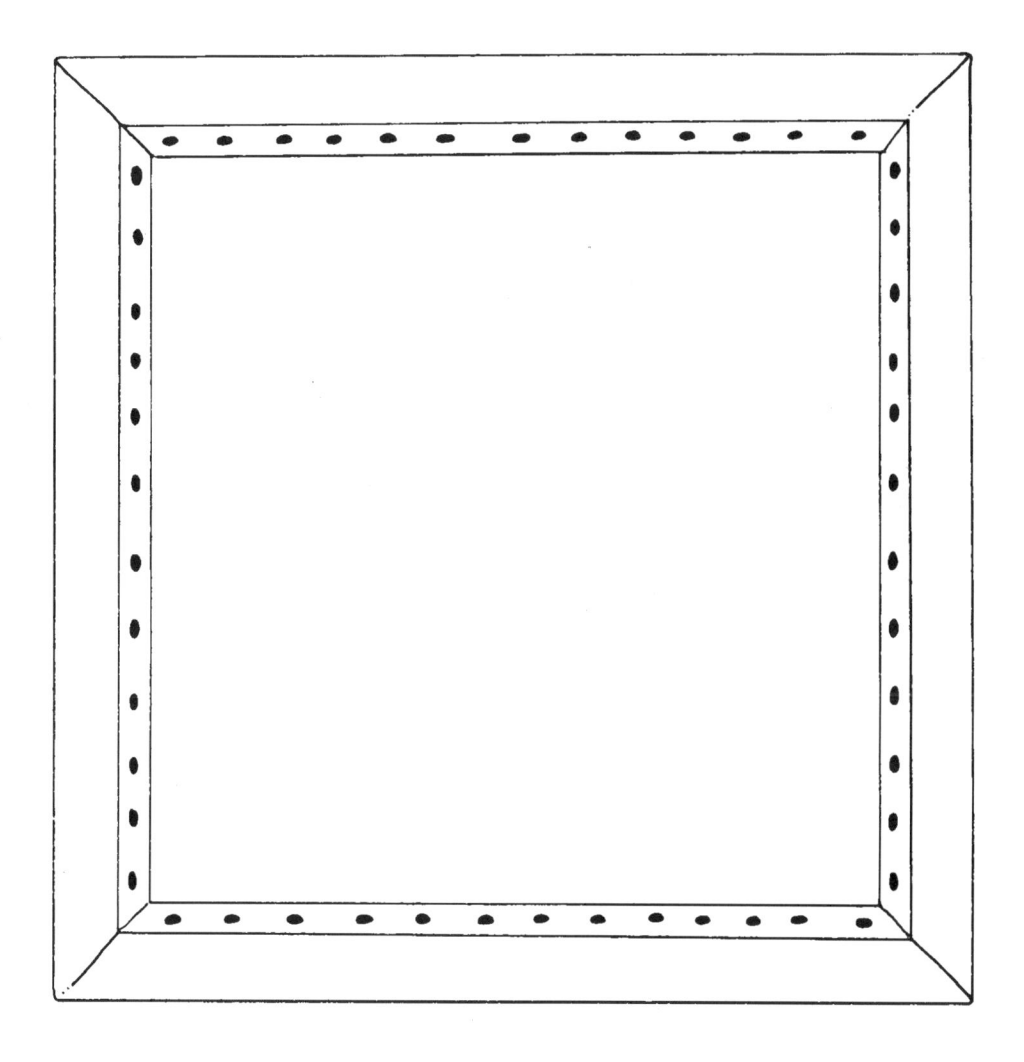

◆ Draw a circle round the words that describe your friend. Write some of your own words.

black hair	curly hair	round face
red hair	straight hair	long face
blonde hair	long hair	square face
brown hair	short hair	

PHOTOCOPIABLE PAGE

◆ We are all different ◆

◆ Write the names of three friends who:

◆ like to read.

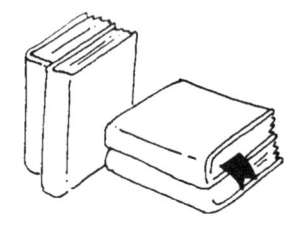

◆ like to play football.

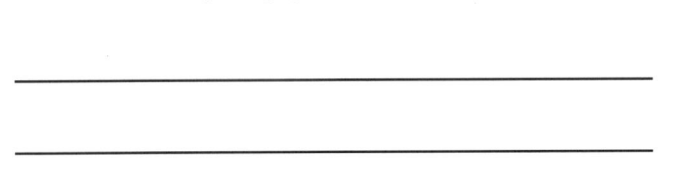

◆ like to write stories.

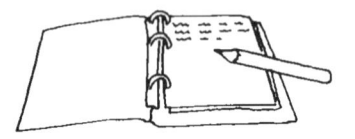

◆ like to draw.

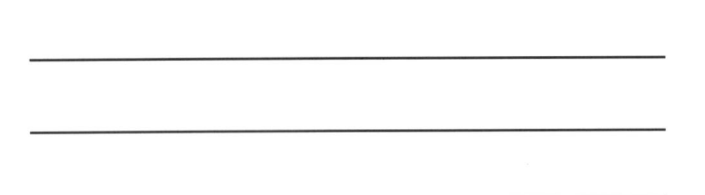

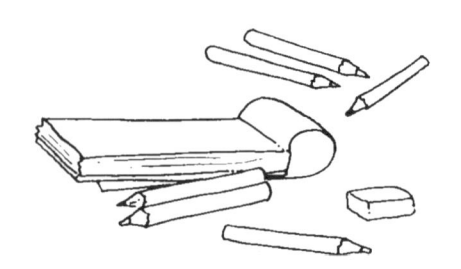

◆ like to listen to music.

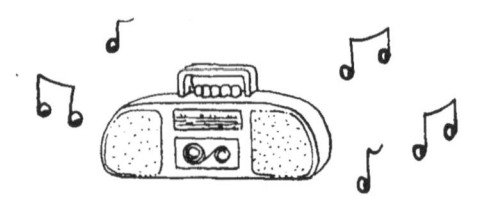

◆ What would they do? ◆

◆ Look at this picture. Imagine this space ship has landed in your playground.

◆ What would you do? Draw yourself in the picture.

◆ Choose two of your friends. Write what you think they would do if this really happened.

Name _____   Name _____

_____   _____

_____   _____

_____   _____

◆ Would you all do something different?

Yes ☐   No ☐

PHOTOCOPIABLE PAGE

15

◆Friendship

FOCUS BOOK
I HATE ROLAND ROBERTS
by Martina Selway
Red Fox (Random House)

INTENDED LEARNING

◆ To understand that friendships have to be built and worked at.

◆ To be open-minded about who they might have friendships with, understanding that first impressions can sometimes be wrong.

ANTICIPATED OUTCOMES

◆ An understanding that friendships are based on shared interests and that people don't necessarily have to be alike to be friends.

Synopsis of the story

Rosie is not at all happy about going to a new school and becomes even more unhappy when the teacher sits her next to a boy called Roland Roberts, who teases her and calls her names. In a long letter to her Grandad, Rosie writes about how horrible Roland is and how much she dislikes him. She is even more horrified when her mother invites Roland and his Mum to tea. It is on this occasion that Roland discovers that his preconceptions about girls are quite wrong. By the end of the story, when the two children have found that they have lots in common, Rosie's feelings have changed.

Notes for teachers

Anyone who works with young children will know how difficult things can get when friendships don't quite work out.

Learning to make relationships with their peers can sometimes be a difficult and painful process and, when things go wrong, children can become very distressed. When this happens it is easy for us to unwittingly trivialise children's feelings by not relating to this distress. We may fail to understand the hurt and isolation they are feeling and may well try to dismiss it with comments like "Don't worry, there are plenty of other people that will be your friend."

By sharing I Hate Roland Roberts with children we are helping them to see that friendships are not always simple and easy and that they can be surprisingly unpredictable. The story demonstrates beautifully that first impressions are not necessarily reliable and that stereotyped ideas about people are not useful. It helps children to see the way in which friendships happen over time and are built on shared interests.

Methodology

Read the story with the children, encouraging them to think about Rosie's feelings.

Questions to ask

- How was Rosie feeling about going to her new school? Why?
- Rosie and Roland were not happy about having to sit together. Why do you think this was?
- Can you think of some words that might describe how Rosie felt when her Mum invited Roland and his Mum to tea? (You may need to introduce words such as horrified, angry, exasperated, frustrated and cross.)
- Have you had to spend time with someone you didn't want to? How does it feel?
- At what point in the story did Roland and Rosie begin to feel differently about each other? What do you think made this happen?
- Look carefully at the page where all the children are playing in the snow. What did Roland say that tells us that he had begun to like Rosie?
- What did Rosie and Roland find out about each other?
- Encourage the children to relate the story to their own experience. Ask "Have you ever started off not liking someone and then made friends with them?", "Have you always had the same friends or have your friends changed?", "What sort of things do you and your friends enjoy doing together?"
- Draw the children's attention to the way the book is written. Ask them "Why do you think Rosie wrote all of this down and sent it to her Grandad?"
- What does Roland say in the end that tells us that he really likes Rosie?
- Children like to feel that they belong to 'the group' and that they can make a contribution to that group. When Rosie first arrived at the school this did not happen. Have the children ever felt left out? You might ask them:
  – "Why do we need friends?"
  – "Why are they important?"
  – "What would it feel like not to have any friends?"
  – "If you had sat next to Rosie on her first day at a new school what would you have done to help her?"

The photocopiable activity sheets

Friends like the same things This sheet is aimed at helping children understand the way in which friends have shared interests. It requires very little writing, although younger children may need some help compiling the list at the bottom of the page.

You and your friends This activity has the same purpose as the previous sheet but requires the children to write a sentence or two independently.

What they like The purpose of this worksheet is to encourage the children to think about the ways in which their friends' likes and dislikes do or do not correspond with their own. It requires a considerable amount of writing and is probably best used with older children.

FURTHER READING

- Mary Mary by Sarah Hayes, illustrated by Helen Craig (Walker Books)
- Pass it, Polly by Sarah Garland (Puffin)

◆ Friends like the same things ◆

◆ Colour the pictures of the things that Rosie and Roland were **both** interested in.

◆ Write the name of one of your friends.

✎ _____

◆ Write a list of some things that you **both** like.

◆ _____   ◆ _____

◆ _____   ◆ _____

◆ _____   ◆ _____

PHOTOCOPIABLE PAGE

◆ You and your friends ◆

◆ Here are some pictures of things that Rosie and Roland both liked to do.

◆ Choose a friend and write and draw about what you both like to do.

My friend's name is _____ .

PHOTOCOPIABLE PAGE

19

◆ What they like ◆

◆ Choose six friends. Complete the chart below.

Name	What they like	What they don't like

◆Families

Synopsis of the story

This is the story of an Afro-Caribbean family on the day of Daddy's birthday. Mum and baby await the arrival of auntie, uncle, cousins, grandmas and finally Daddy, so that they can all join in celebrating his birthday.

Notes for teachers

This is an amazing book full of tenderness and humour that tells of the way in which all baby's relations love him in their own special way. The illustrations are stunning and support the text beautifully, providing us with a wonderful springboard for the exploration of family life.

So Much will really help the children in appreciating and understanding the way in which families are made up of different people who all offer love and support to children in different ways.

The family in the story enjoys spending time together and presents the reader with a model of family celebration. In exploring the issues around the story, it is essential that we consider our definition of 'family' as not all children will have experiences of the nuclear family. In this context we take 'family' to be the supportive close community in which we live and this may mean different things to different people. For example, some children may live with only one parent, with grandparents or with foster carers.

FOCUS BOOK

SO MUCH
by Trish Cooke
and Helen Oxenbury
Walker Books

INTENDED LEARNING

◆ To understand the family as a source of love and support important to our well-being.
◆ To help our children understand that families can be different.

ANTICIPATED OUTCOMES

◆ The children will be able to identify and talk about the ways in which families can offer us love and support.
◆ They will understand that not all families are the same and will be able to talk about the ways in which they are different.

Methodology

It might be worth clarifying the children's perceptions of what the book is about. They may say "It's about Daddy's birthday" and while this is true, we need to lead them to an understanding of the book's wider meaning.

Questions to ask

- Turn to the front page and ask:
  - How are Mum and Baby feeling?
  - Why are they looking out of the window?
- Why does Auntie Bibba want to squeeze the baby? The word squeeze can be associated with hurting someone. Through discussion, encourage the children to identify the difference.
- How did Auntie Bibba play with the baby? The children should understand that the baby's family all play with him and express their love in different ways.
- How did Uncle Didi play with the baby? How did the baby feel?
- What do Nannie and Gran-Gran do with the baby? Do they really want to eat him? Has anyone ever said this to you?
- At this point it may be worth asking the children why some of the pictures have almost no colour on them. What is the illustrator trying to show?
- How does cousin Kay-Kay play with the baby? How does the baby feel about this?
- To help the children understand the ways in which people are different, ask them to look at the page just before Dad arrives. Ask "What are all the different people doing to help pass the time?"
- When Daddy comes home, do you think he is expecting all the family to be there?
- How do you think Daddy feels when he sees all the people there?
- Point out that everybody there felt that it was important to wait for Daddy to come home from work so that they could spend time with him on his birthday.
- How did Daddy play with the baby?
- Even though the baby was very young, he could tell that his family loved him. How do people show that they love you? Encourage the children to talk about their own families and share experiences of family celebrations.

The photocopiable activity sheets

Make a family This is a cut and paste activity aimed at encouraging the children to think about the ways in which families are different. It requires little writing and is suitable for the younger children. It has the potential to lead to some interesting discussion about different sorts of families.

Families are important In this activity the children are asked to reflect upon members of their family and why they are important to them. It requires very little writing and can be enhanced by providing the children with an opportunity for comparing their sheets and discussing the commonalities.

Showing love This sheet asks children to write about a picture and then write about their own family. It is intended for children who can write independently.

FURTHER READING

- Peace at Last and Five Minutes' Peace by Jill Murphy (PictureMac)
- Once There Were Giants by Martin Waddell (Walker Books)
- John Joe and the Big Hen by Martin Waddell, illustrated by Paul Howard (Walker Books)
- Alfie's Feet by Shirley Hughes (Picture Lions)
- When Willy Went to the Wedding by Judith Kerr (Picture Lions)

◆ Make a family ◆

◆ Choose some people from the pictures below to make a family. Cut out their pictures and stick them on to a sheet of paper. Write who they are.

PHOTOCOPIABLE PAGE

◆ Families are important ◆

◆ Draw yourself in the middle. Then draw some of the people in your family and write their names.

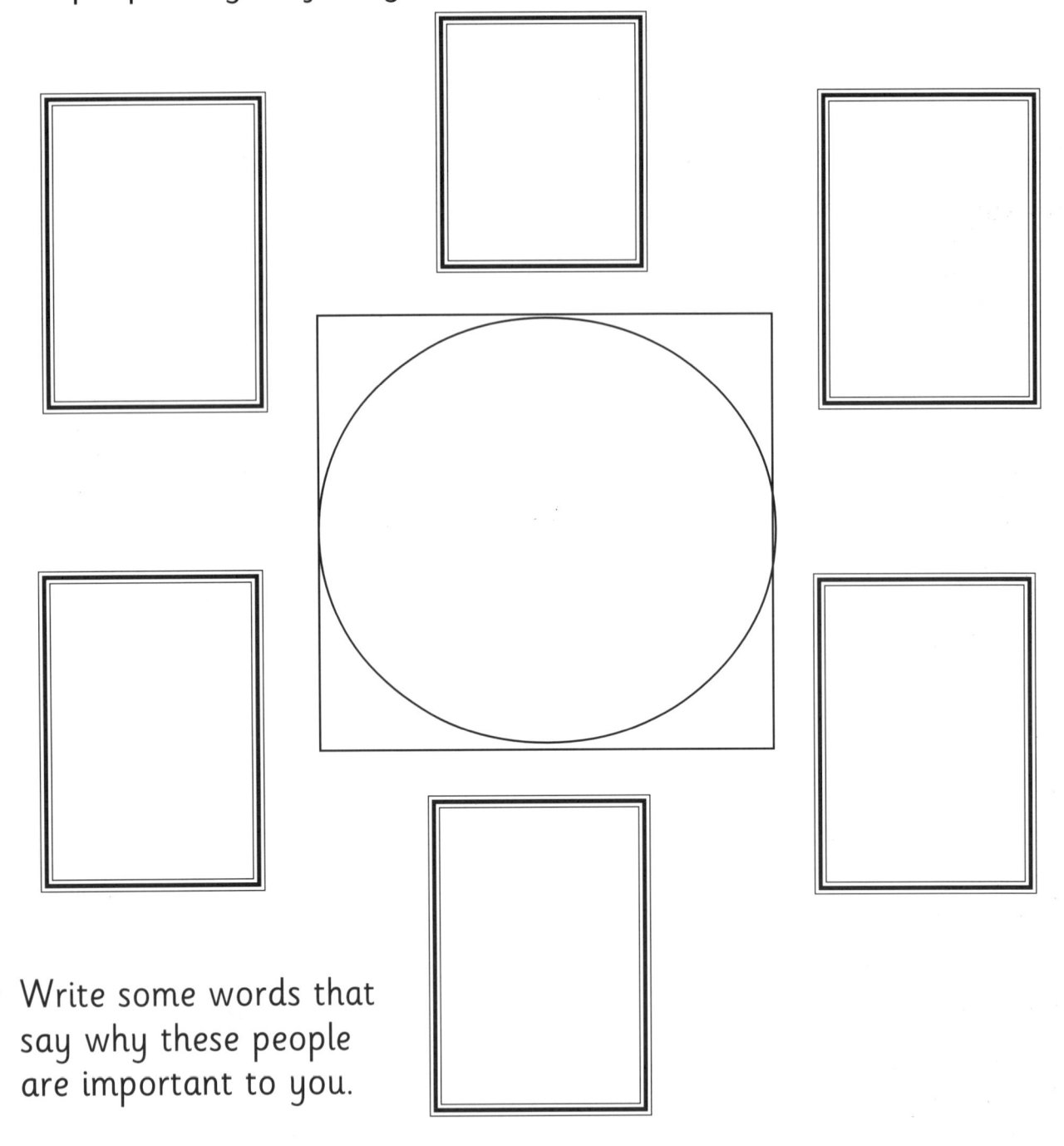

◆ Write some words that say why these people are important to you.

PHOTOCOPIABLE PAGE

◆ Showing love ◆

◆ Write about what is happening in this picture.

_____
_____
_____
_____
_____

◆ Draw a picture to show one of the ways in which your family loves you. Write a few words about your family.

_____
_____
_____
_____

PHOTOCOPIABLE PAGE

Brothers and sisters

FOCUS BOOK

THE TUNNEL
by Anthony Browne
Walker Books

INTENDED LEARNING

- ◆ To understand that not all siblings get on well together.
- ◆ To see that you don't have to be alike in order to love and respect someone.

ANTICIPATED OUTCOMES

- ◆ The children will be able to talk about the different kinds of relationships that exist between children within the same family.
- ◆ They will appreciate diversity within these relationships and know that love and respect can exist within a range of differing situations.

Synopsis of the story

Although Jack and Rose are brother and sister they have little in common. They don't enjoy spending time together and fight and argue all the time. It is not until their mother forces them to go out together and Rose senses that Jack is in danger that their real feelings for each other emerge. In spite of 'feelings of intense fear', Rose crawls through a slimy tunnel to help her brother.

Notes for teachers

This is an excellent story for illustrating the way in which siblings, who appear to have little affection for each other, can display enormous loyalty and commitment when something happens to threaten one of them. It can help children to understand that brothers and sisters who don't always get on well together can still love each other.

There is an expectation that because children come from the same family they will like each other and want to spend time together. When this does not happen, the children can feel that something is wrong and even develop feelings of guilt about the situation. The Tunnel is a really good springboard for the exploration of feelings between siblings and helps to show that children from the same family are individuals who can be very different and have different interests.

It is important to be aware of those children who have no brothers and sisters and to ensure that they are not left out of the discussion. They will not have a personal perspective of the situation but they will have other opinions and comments to bring to the lesson.

Methodology

The story raises questions relating to the nature of families. Within any class, children will come from a range of different families and it is important to help them recognise that the love and commitment required for a secure and happy childhood can be found in families of different kinds. With this in mind it may be useful to engage in a general discussion about families.

Questions to ask

- How do Rose and Jack feel about each other? What happens when they are together? Encourage children to relate this to their own experiences by asking:
  - How do you feel about your brothers and sisters?
  - What do you like and not like about them?
- Sometimes Jack crept into Rose's room at night. He wanted to scare her even though he knew she was afraid of the dark. Has your brother or sister ever done anything like that to you? Have you ever done that to your brother or sister?
- How did Mum feel about Jack and Rose? She made them go out together. Why?
- Rose did not want to go into the tunnel. Can you think of some words to describe her feelings when her brother went into the tunnel and left her?
- When he didn't come back, the story tells us that 'she had to follow him into the tunnel'. Why was it important for Rose to do this, especially when she was so frightened? What would you have done?
- When Rose comes out of the tunnel, she finds herself in a wood. (At this point, take time to allow the children to observe and discuss the amazing illustrations.)
- When Rose sees the figure still as stone, she sobs, thinking she is too late. Ask them to think of some words that would describe Rose's feelings.
- Why did Rose throw her arms around Jack?
- Why do you think he 'came back to life'? This is a subtle metaphor for the children, but with some encouragement, they may grasp its meaning.
- Jack told Rose that he knew she would come. Why was he so sure?
- How had things changed for Jack and Rose when they got home?

The photocopiable activity sheets

Your brother and sister This activity provides the children with an opportunity for focusing on a brother or sister and reflecting upon the sort of things that interest them. It requires no writing but could promote discussion around whether the children's interests were the same or different from those of their brother or sister.

What would you do? In this activity the children are asked to think about how they would respond if their brother or sister was in danger. It will need to be preceded by plenty of discussion.

Other brothers and sisters This activity is intended for children who can write independently. In implementing it the childen should be encouraged to see that we all possess a range of attributes and that no-one can be 100% likeable all of the time.

FURTHER READING

- Titch and You'll Soon Grow Into Them, Titch by Pat Hutchins (Picture Puffins)

◆ Your brother or sister ◆

◆ Draw a picture of your brother or sister. If you don't have one, draw a picture of one that you would like to have.

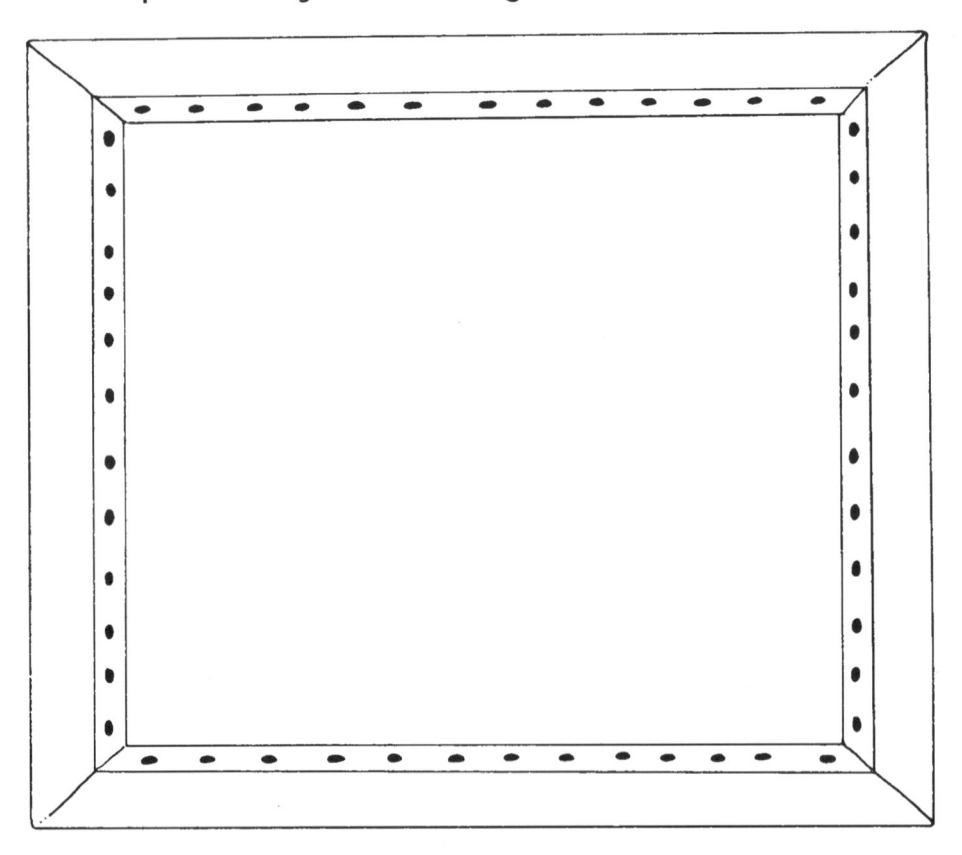

◆ Look at the words below. Put a ✔ by the things that interest your brother or sister.

football ☐   computers ☐   swimming ☐

books ☐   animals ☐   music ☐

television ☐   dancing ☐   drawing ☐

◆ Write some words of your own.

PHOTOCOPIABLE PAGE

◆ What would you do? ◆

◆ Imagine your brother or sister is in danger. What would you do? Draw yourself in this picture.

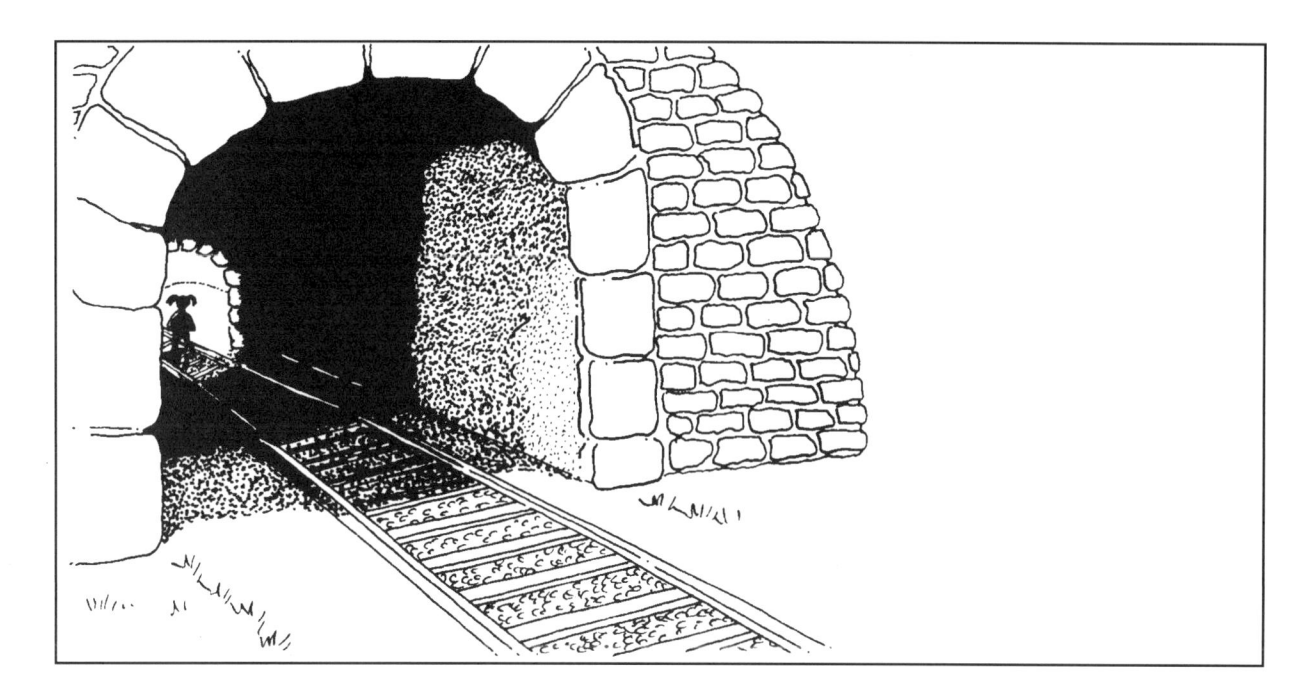

◆ Imagine this is your brother or sister. Write what you think might happen to them.

◆ Think of some words to describe how you would feel about going into the tunnel. Write them in the boxes.

PHOTOCOPIABLE PAGE

Other brothers and sisters

◆ Interview someone who has a brother or sister.

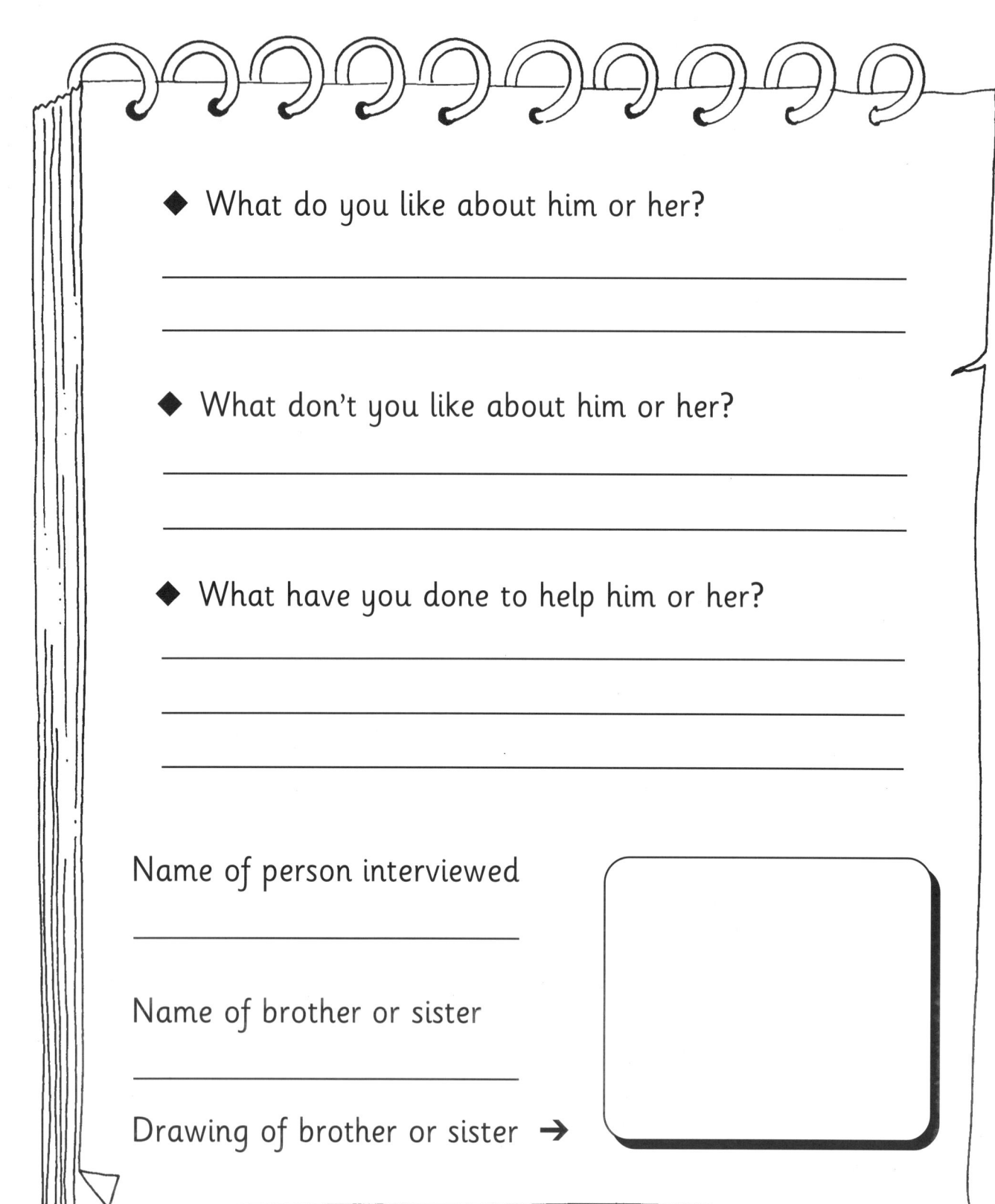

◆ What do you like about him or her?

_____
_____

◆ What don't you like about him or her?

_____
_____

◆ What have you done to help him or her?

_____
_____
_____

Name of person interviewed

_____

Name of brother or sister

_____

Drawing of brother or sister →

◆Responsibilities

FOCUS BOOK

JOHN JOE AND THE BIG HEN
by Martin Waddell
and Paul Howard
Walker Books

INTENDED LEARNING

◆ To understand we all have responsibilities and that sometimes they give rise to a conflict of interests.
◆ To understand that there are consequences to us failing in our responsibilities.

ANTICIPATED OUTCOMES

◆ The children will know that responsibility is part of belonging and that it can involve a conflict of interests.
◆ They will be able to think about the consequences of not taking their responsibilities seriously.

Synopsis of the story

Mary and her brother Sammy have to take it in turns to look after their little brother John Joe and when it is Sammy's turn he is not keen! He decides that he would much rather play with his friends and runs off to the Brennan's farm leaving John Joe in the yard. His sister Mary is outraged at his behaviour and taking John Joe with her, follows Sammy to the farm. When they get there the farm is deserted. Leaving John Joe in the farm yard, Mary goes to the stream to look for Sammy. While alone in the yard, John Joe is intimidated by the Brennan's big hen and runs away, finally taking refuge in the corn field. When Mary returns with Sammy they are horrified to find John Joe missing but with the help of Splinter the dog they find him fast asleep in the corn.

Notes for teachers

Many children will have experience of minding a younger brother or sister and the conflict of interests that can result from such a situation. John Joe and the Big Hen is an excellent vehicle for the exploration of family responsibilities. It also affords us the opportunity to examine the feelings of resentment that may arise when we feel that one member of the family is not doing their fair share.

Learning to take our responsibilities seriously is not always easy, but in sharing this book with children we can allow them time to reflect on this process and consider the feelings of guilt that can be experienced when we fall short of meeting our responsibilities.

Methodology

Read the story with the children.

Questions to ask

- Can you think of some words that would describe Sammy's feelings when he realised it was his turn to look after John Joe?
- How did Mary feel when Sammy ran off, leaving her with John Joe?
- What did Mary do when she found herself with John Joe? Why did she do this?
- Why did Mary leave John Joe at the farm on his own?
- When John Joe was left on his own he was frightened by Mrs Brennan's big hen. How did he deal with this?
- By the time Mary came back with Sammy and Splinter, John Joe was nowhere to be seen. How do you think they felt? What thoughts might have been going through their heads? (This may be a good time to introduce vocabulary such as anxious, concerned, worried, guilty and panic.)
- Look at the picture on the last page. What do you think Mary and Sammy are thinking? What do you think Mammy will say to them?
- Do you think what Sammy did was right? What should he have done when his Mammy said that it was his turn to look after John Joe?
- Mary felt angry. Was she right to feel that way?
- Have you ever had to look after a brother or sister when you really wanted to do something else? What did that feel like? (Allow the children to share ideas and experiences. It is important to help them understand that conflict is a natural part of life. We cannot avoid conflict and should not feel guilty about it. What is important is that we respond consciously and appropriately to such situations.)
- Encourage them to see the concept of personal responsibility in a wider context. Ask about their responsibilities at home, such as feeding pets or washing up, and at school. How do they feel about this? What happens if people do not carry out their responsibilities.
- Discuss responsibility in relation to adults. What sort of responsibilities do your parents/carers/teachers have? (Encourage the children to see the connection between responsibility and our relationships with others and encourage them to see that carrying out our responsibilities is an important part of relationships.)

The photocopiable activity sheets

What will happen? This is a speaking and listening activity designed to promote discussion around acting responsibly. It does not involve any written work.

Doing jobs In this activity the children are asked to think about why it is important for them to help with household chores. They need to be able to write short sentences independently.

Who does what? This sheet encourages the children to explore and compare their respective responsibilities. To complete the sheet independently they need to be able to write without assistance, although younger children could do the activity with the help of an adult.

FURTHER READING

- Mamo on the Mountain by Jane Kurtz and E B Lewis (Gollancz Children's Paperback)

What will happen?

◆ Read this story. In the two empty boxes, draw pictures to show what you think will happen. Use speech bubbles if you want to.

PHOTOCOPIABLE PAGE

◆ Doing jobs ◆

◆ What is happening in the picture?

✏️ _____

_____

◆ Why do you think this is happening?

✏️ _____

_____

◆ What jobs do you have to do at home?

◆ _____ ◆ _____

◆ _____ ◆ _____

◆ Who does what? ◆

◆ Talk to three of your friends about the jobs they do at home. Are they the same as yours?

My name	Responsibilities
Name of friend	Responsibilities
Name of friend	Responsibilities
Name of friend	Responsibilities

Listening to each other

FOCUS BOOK

NOT NOW, BERNARD
by David McKee
Andersen Press

INTENDED LEARNING

◆ To be aware of the importance of listening and the range of skills required for good listening.

ANTICIPATED OUTCOMES

◆ The children will understand that listening is not just about hearing. They will know that it requires a range of skills that need to be practised and developed.

◆ They will be able to talk about some of the pre-requisites for good listening.

Synopsis of the story

Bernard tries hard to tell his parents about the monster in the garden, but they are far too busy to listen to him. Unfortunately, when Bernard goes out into the garden the monster gobbles him up. When the monster goes into the house, he also finds that no-one will take any notice of him. Bernard's parents are so absorbed in what they are doing they assume that Bernard has returned, so the monster plays with Bernard's toys, eats Bernard's tea and gets sent to bed by Bernard's mother. The story ends with Bernard's mother switching off the light, still unaware of what has happened to her son.

Notes for teachers

As teachers, although we are constantly urging children to listen carefully, we probably spend far too little time actually teaching them how to do it. Listening involves distinct skills that can be both taught and evaluated. Listening is an active process requiring our participation and simply being quiet while someone is talking does not constitute real listening.

Through exploring the issues raised in Not Now Bernard, we can raise children's awareness of the importance of listening and help them understand that listening skills can be developed.

Real listening is based on the intention to do one of four things:
◆ understand someone   ◆ learn something   ◆ give help
◆ appreciate someone

It involves us in concentrating, paraphrasing, clarifying and giving feedback and is important for:
◆ good communication   ◆ enjoyment of literature and the media
◆ effective relationships   ◆ understanding and following instructions
◆ discussion   ◆ reasoning

We all appreciate being listened to. By developing our listening skills we can reach a greater awareness of ourselves and others, improve our relationships and increase our capacity for learning.

Methodology

In discussing the story the following questions and points for consideration may prove helpful:

◆ Encourage the children to look carefully at the pictures of Bernard attempting to communicate with his parents. Discuss what is happening by asking:
- How can you tell when no-one is listening to Bernard?
- Why do you think Bernard's parents took no notice of him?
- Is there anything else Bernard could have said to make his parents listen?

◆ Encourage the children to relate this to their own experience by asking:
- Has anything like this ever happened to you?
- What does it feel like when someone doesn't listen to you?
- Would Bernard have been eaten by the monster if his parents had listened to him?
- When the monster roars at Bernard's mother what does she think is happening? With the children, look at the monster's facial expressions both before and after he has roared at Bernard's mother.

◆ When the monster bites Bernard's father, what does he think is going on? Here again it might be worth getting the children to examine the pictures and talk about the monster's feelings.

◆ In the time between dinner time and bed time nobody communicates with the monster. To help the children appreciate this ask:
- What did the monster do after he had eaten Bernard's dinner?
- Did anyone speak to him while he was doing these things?
- How do you think the monster felt about this?
- How would you feel if this happened to you?

◆ The monster goes to bed. How does he feel about what is happening to him? Why does he feel this way?

◆ When Bernard's Mum switches off the light, she still doesn't know what has happened to him. What do you think would happen the next day?

◆ Draw the children's attention to the way in which, in some pictures the adults eyes are open, whereas in some they are closed. Ask the children if they can give a reason for this.

◆ Encourage the children to relate the story to their own experience by asking:
- Have you ever tried to talk to someone who didn't listen to you?
- What did you do when this happened?
- What things do you need to do to be a good listener?

The photocopiable activity sheets

Find the good listener As teachers we are always telling children to listen carefully! This activity requires no writing and is aimed at encouraging the children to think about what we have to do to be good listeners.

What is a good listener? This sheet is an extension of the previous one and asks the children to define and list the characteristics of good listening.

What could happen? This activity involves the children in thinking about the consequences of not listening. They need to be able to write independently.

FURTHER READING

◆ **The Wild Baby** by Barbro Lindgren, pictures by Eva Eriksch (Hippo Books)

◆ Find the good listener ◆

◆ Look carefully at these pictures. Colour the picture where someone is listening.

◆ Write some words about the picture you have coloured.

_____

_____

PHOTOCOPIABLE PAGE

◆ What is a good listener? ◆

◆ Look at these two pictures.

◆ Write a list of things that help us to be good listeners.

◆
◆
◆
◆
◆
◆

◆ Write a list of things that people do when they are not good listeners.

◆
◆
◆
◆
◆
◆

PHOTOCOPIABLE PAGE

◆ What could happen? ◆

◆ Write what you think could happen.

✎ _____

_____

◆ How will the two men feel?

✎ _____

_____

◆ Think of some other times when it is important that we listen. Write about one of them here.

✎ _____

_____

PHOTOCOPIABLE PAGE

Loss and how to cope

FOCUS BOOK
COME BACK, GRANDMA
by Sue limb
and Claudio Munoz
Red Fox (Random House)

INTENDED LEARNING

◆ To understand that death is something that is both natural and inevitable.
◆ To understand that there are some questions for which we simply do not have the answers.

ANTICIPATED OUTCOMES

◆ The children will understand that death is something that will happen to all of us.
◆ They will understand that grief is quite natural.
◆ They will be able to talk openly about death.

Synopsis of the story

Bessie loves her Mum and Dad very much, but they always seem so busy. Her brother is still a baby and no fun to play with, but Grandma . . . Grandma is very special. She always has time for Bessie and is happy to join in all her games and help her to learn new things, until one day Grandma becomes ill and dies. The rest of the story deals with Bessie's sadness, which is never finally resolved until she grows up and has a daughter just like Grandma.

Notes for teachers

Come Back, Grandma is an excellent picture book about death and a marvellous vehicle through which we may address this difficult issue with very young children.

We live in a society where death can be a taboo subject and where children in particular are shielded from it in a way that is not always useful. This may be done with the best of intentions but does not help us in dealing with a process that is both natural and inevitable. As with birth, death is an experience that we will all eventually share and one over which we have absolutely no control. Looked at in this way, it seems nonsensical that it is also an experience that most of us ignore until it impacts on us personally through the death of someone close to us.

With advances in medical science, we are living much longer, so many of us may be adults before we experience such a loss. The secularisation of society has further complicated the exploration of this sensitive issue. Until fairly recently, belief in an after-life was common; we now have additional difficulties in answering questions about what happens to us when we die.

Death is now more sanitised than it used to be with more people dying in hospital and less dying at home. There is a preference for cremation over burial which means that we are less likely to experience the finality of a coffin being buried in the ground. Such circumstances do little to prepare us for coping with the feelings that engulf us when someone close to us dies, but through sharing and discussing Come Back, Grandma with children we can help them to begin to understand death and perhaps address issues that may be troubling them.

Methodology

The discussion of this book calls for great sensitivity on the part of the teacher and there are some important factors to be taken into consideration:
◆ Any child who has been recently bereaved should be able to opt out of the lesson.
◆ This work is perhaps not best carried out by a teacher who has experienced recent bereavement.

Questions to ask

Ensure that there is plenty of time for discussion. The children will raise many questions for themselves and some of the following questions may prove useful:
◆ Bessie had a very special relationship with her Grandma. Why do you think she liked her Grandma so much? The children may then want to talk about their own grandparents and the things that they do with them.
◆ How did Bessie feel when her Grandma got ill and died? Try to get the children to extend the range of feelings beyond sad and upset. It may be useful to introduce words such as confused, lonely, lost and anxious.
◆ Bessie missed Grandma a lot. What do you think she missed most?
◆ Bessie's Mum said that Grandma had gone to heaven. Share ideas about what heaven is. Explain that there will be lots of different ideas about it.
◆ Bessie asks if Grandma will be able to phone from heaven but she doesn't get an answer. Ask the children what they think. This should help them in understanding the permanence of death.
◆ Khriona says that Grandma might be born again as an animal or a bird. Introduce the idea of reincarnation and other beliefs.
◆ Even when Bessie grew up she sometimes missed Grandma. Why?
◆ When Bessie grew up she had a little girl and called her Rose. As Rose grew up, what did Bessie notice about her? How did she feel about this?
◆ Encourage the children to relate the story to their own experience. Have they ever loved anyone who has died? If they have not experienced the death of a person they might have had a pet that has died. Allow them time to talk about their feelings at the time and the practical things they did, such as burying the pet in the garden or making a cross or other symbol.

The photocopiable activity sheets

Time line This is aimed at younger children. It requires no writing and is a sequencing activity to help them think about the process of growing older.

How could you help? This activity is designed to get children thinking about how they might support a friend whose pet has died. It will need quite a lot of discussion, especially around why it would not be a good idea to leave the friend alone or tell him he will soon forget.

Losing someone you love This activity focuses on the loss of a grandparent. It is intended for children who can discuss issues with greater sophistication and who can write independently.

FURTHER READING

◆ My Grandad by S Isherwood, illustrations by Kate Isherwood (Oxford Children's Books)

◆ Time line ◆

◆ We all grow and change. Cut out these pictures and put them in the right order.

PHOTOCOPIABLE PAGE

◆ How could you help? ◆

◆ Look at this picture. What has happened?

◆ What could you do to help? Put a ✔ in the boxes.

Take him home. ☐   Leave him alone. ☐

Tell him he will soon forget. ☐   Give him a cuddle. ☐

◆ Draw a picture and write a few words about someone whose pet died.

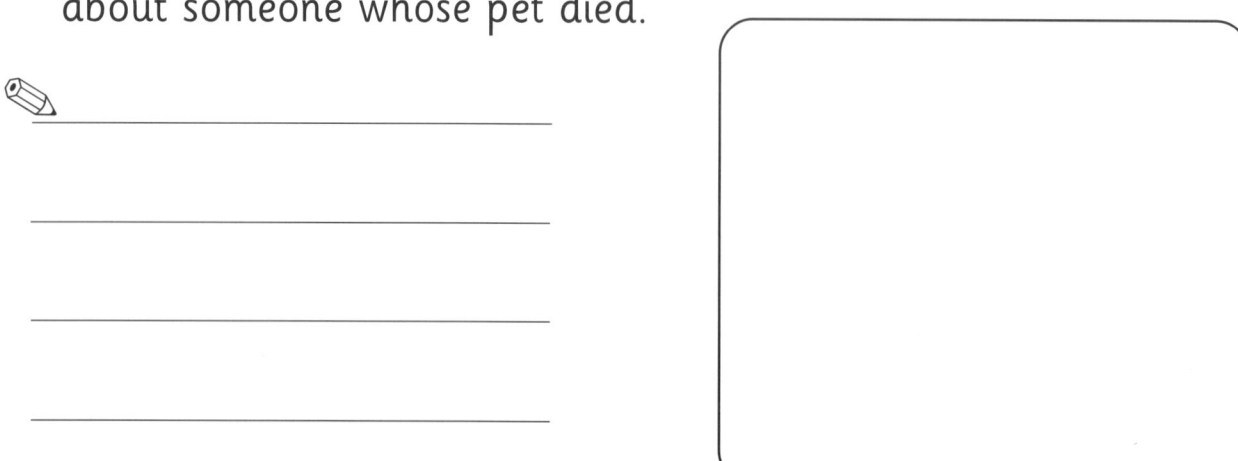

PHOTOCOPIABLE PAGE

◆ Losing someone you love ◆

◆ Look at this picture of two children with their grandparents.

◆ Imagine that one of the grandparents dies. How would the children feel about it?

✎ _____

_____

◆ What things might they remember about their grandparent?

✎ _____

_____

◆ What could you say to help them?

✎ _____

_____

◆ Who helps us? ◆

◆ Look at these pictures. Draw some more pictures about helping people. Write their names.

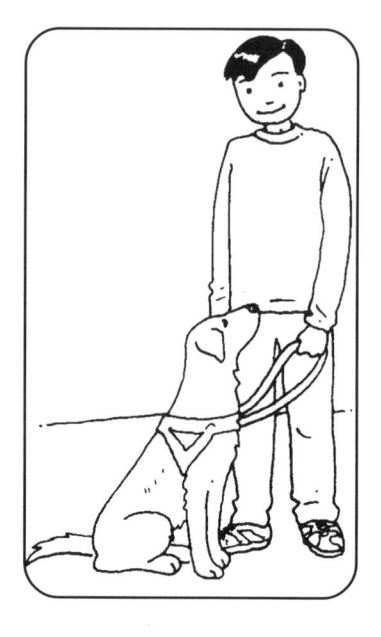

Name _____

Name _____

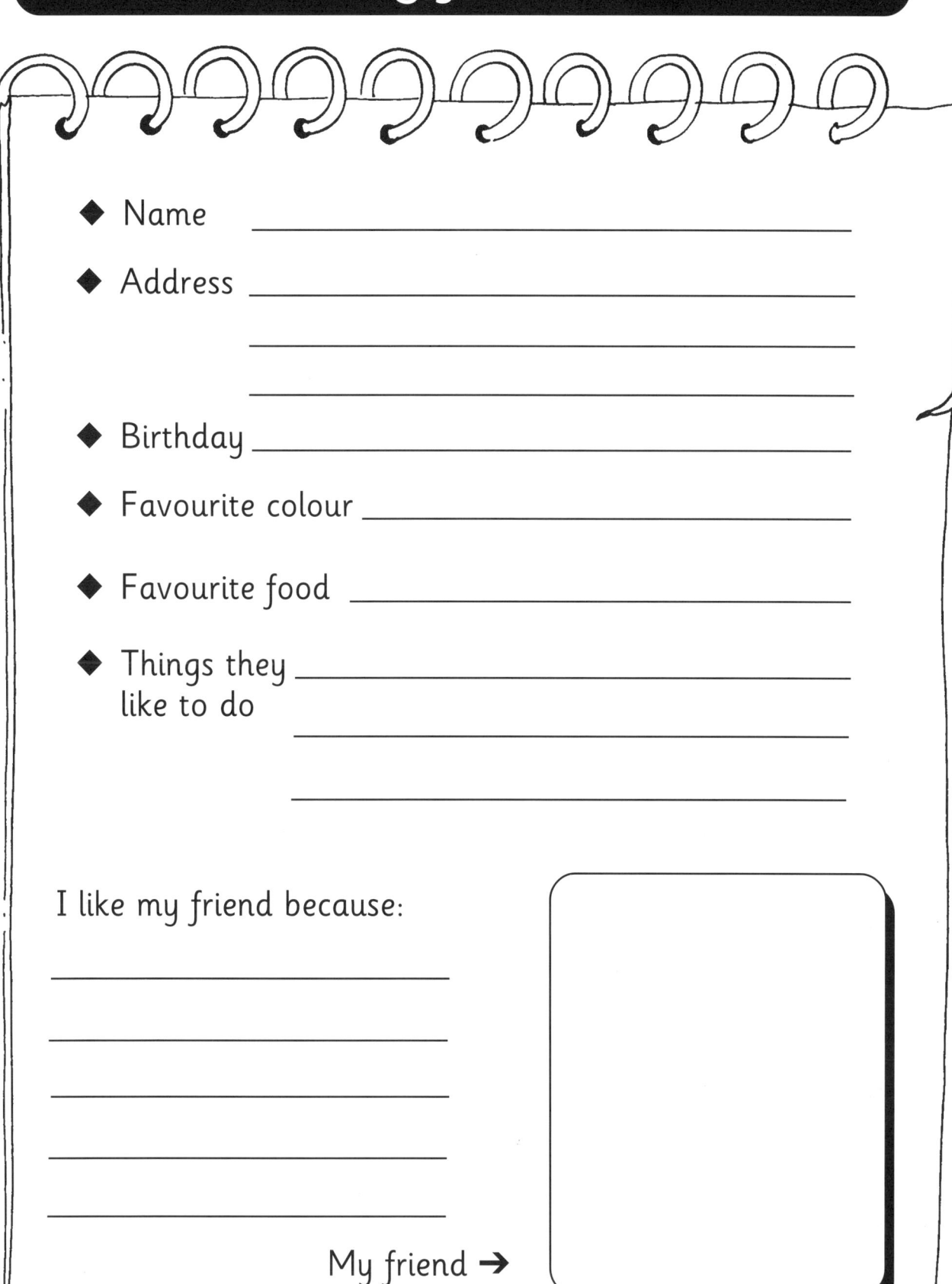

◆ My friend ◆

- ◆ Name _____
- ◆ Address _____
  _____
  _____
- ◆ Birthday _____
- ◆ Favourite colour _____
- ◆ Favourite food _____
- ◆ Things they like to do _____
  _____
  _____

I like my friend because:

_____
_____
_____
_____

My friend →

PHOTOCOPIABLE PAGE